Pebble®

Great African-Americans

Wilma
RUDOLPH

by Isabel Martin   Consulting Editor: Gail Saunders-Smith, PhD

CAPSTONE PRESS
a capstone imprint

Pebble Books are published by Capstone Press,
1710 Roe Crest Drive, North Mankato, Minnesota 56003
www.capstonepub.com

Library of Congress Cataloging-in-Publication Data
Martin, Isabel, 1977–
  Wilma Rudolph / by Isabel Martin.
     pages cm.—(Pebble books. Great African-Americans)
  Includes bibliographical references and index.
  Summary: "Simple text and photographs present the life of Wilma Rudolph, the first American
woman to win three Olympic gold medals"—Provided by publisher.
  ISBN 978-1-4914-0503-1 (library binding)—ISBN 978-1-4914-0509-3 (paperback)—
  ISBN 978-1-4914-0515-4 (ebook PDF)
  1. Rudolph, Wilma, 1940—Juvenile literature. 2. Runners (Sports)—United States—Biography—
Juvenile literature. 3. Women runners—United States—Biography—Juvenile literature. I. Title.
  GV1061.15.R83M37 2015
  796.42092—dc23
  [B]   2013049778

Editorial Credits
Nikki Bruno Clapper, editor; Terri Poburka, designer; Kelly Garvin, media researcher;
Laura Manthe, production specialist

Photo Credits
AP Images, 6, 10; Corbis: Bettmann, 14, 18, Jerry Cooke, 12; Getty Images: Bob Thomas,
4, Denver Post, 20, Time & Life Pictures, cover, 8; Glow Images/Everett Collection, 16;
Shutterstock/Bule Sky Photo, cover art

Note to Parents and Teachers

The Great African-Americans set supports national curriculum standards for
social studies related to people, places, and environments. This book describes and
illustrates Wilma Rudolph. The images support early readers in understanding the
text. The repetition of words and phrases helps early readers learn new words.
This book also introduces early readers to subject-specific vocabulary words, which
are defined in the Glossary section. Early readers may need assistance to read
some words and to use the Table of Contents, Glossary, Read More, Internet Sites,
Critical Thinking Using the Common Core, and Index sections of the book.

Printed in the United States of America in Stevens Point, Wisconsin.
032014   008092WZF14

Table of Contents

Meet Wilma

Wilma Rudolph was a
famous Olympic track
runner from Tennessee.
She was very fast.
People called her the
Tennessee Tornado.

Wilma (right)
with her sister

1940

born

Wilma was born in 1940. As a child, she was sick a lot. Wilma lost the use of her left leg. Doctors said she might not walk again. She wore a leg brace for eight years.

Doctors at this hospital helped Wilma with her leg.

1940

born

Growing Up

Wilma worked hard to get better. Her family helped her. She went to a doctor twice a week. At age 12, Wilma stopped wearing the brace.

Wilma (second from left) with her Olympic teammates

1940
born

1956
runs in Australia
Olympics

By age 16, Wilma was

a track star. She tried out

for the Olympic track team.

She made it! Wilma ran

in the 1956 Olympics

in Australia. She won

a bronze medal.

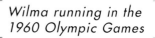

Wilma running in the 1960 Olympic Games

1940
born

1956
runs in Australia
Olympics

1960
runs in Italy
Olympics

Adult Years

Wilma started college
in 1958. She kept
practicing her running.
She wanted to do better
in the next Olympics.
In 1960 she ran in the
Olympic Games in Italy.

1940	**1956**	**1960**
born	runs in Australia Olympics	runs in Italy Olympics; wins three gold medals

Wilma won three
gold medals in Italy.
She was the first
American woman to
win three gold medals
at the same Olympics.

President Kennedy was proud of Wilma.

1940	**1956**	**1960**
born	runs in Australia Olympics	runs in Italy Olympics; wins three gold medals

People were proud
of Wilma. Her hometown
held a parade and a dinner.
The Tennessee Tornado was
the world's most famous
female athlete.

Wilma (right) coaching her daughter Yolanda

1940
born

1956
runs in Australia Olympics

1960
runs in Italy Olympics; wins three gold medals

Later in Life

Wilma graduated from college in 1963. She later got married and had four children. Wilma became a teacher and a track coach. She was named to several different halls of fame.

1963

graduates from college

1940

born

1956

runs in Australia
Olympics

1960

runs in Italy Olympics;
wins three gold medals

In 1981 Wilma started a
group to help young athletes.
She taught them to work
hard like she did. Wilma
died in 1994. People
remember her as a hero.

1963
graduates from
college

1981
starts group for
young athletes

1994
dies

Glossary

bronze medal—a third-place prize

college—a school that students attend after high school

gold medal—a first-place prize

graduate—to finish all the required classes at a school

hall of fame—a place where important people are honored

hero—someone who has courage, strength, and does things that other people can't do

leg brace—a device attached to a leg to pull it into position and make it straight

Olympic—part of the Olympics, a contest of many sports held every four years in a different country

tornado—a violent, spinning column of air that looks like a funnel; Wilma was fast like a tornado

track—a sport where athletes run, jump, and throw

Read More

Herzog, Brad. *G Is for Gold Medal: An Olympic Alphabet.* Ann Arbor, Mich.: Sleeping Bear Press, 2011.

Johnson, Robin. *Take Off Track and Field.* Sports Starters. New York: Crabtree Pub. Company, 2013.

Wade, Mary Dodson. *Amazing Olympic Athlete Wilma Rudolph.* Amazing Americans. Berkeley Heights, N.J.: Enslow Publishers, 2010.

Internet Sites

FactHound offers a safe, fun way to find Internet sites related to this book. All of the sites on FactHound have been researched by our staff.

Here's all you do:
Visit *www.facthound.com*
Type in this code: 9781491405031

Super-cool stuff!

Check out projects, games and lots more at
www.capstonekids.com

Critical Thinking Using the Common Core

1. What happened to Wilma's left leg when she was a child? How did she get better? (Key Ideas and Details)

2. Why do you think people called Wilma the Tennessee Tornado? (Integration of Knowledge and Ideas)

Index

Word Count: 248

Grade: 1

Early-Intervention Level: 20